Introdu

C000214016

The south-western corner of Wales has a
with any other in the British Isles. From
to the ancient oaks of Lawrenny; from the catl
conviviality of Tenby and from the mellow rei
___y at Porthgain to
an almost forgotten but beautiful tower house at Angle there is something for every
walker to enjoy, all enveloped in very fine scenery, with views you will not want to
leave and beaches the whole family can enjoy.

Any of the walks in this book can be undertaken by a reasonably active person,
with **Walks 1** & **3** being the most challenging. Walking boots or strong shoes are
recommended for all of them, and *please* keep in mind that this is farming country
– *dogs must be kept on a lead AT ALL TIMES (or left behind).*

The location of each route is shown on the back cover, and a full summary of
the major characteristics and length of each is described on a special chart inside.
An estimated time for each walk is also given, but for those who enjoy fine views
and like to linger over them, or to further explore history and heritage, it is best to
allow longer. This splendid environment is far too good to hurry through.

Each walk has a map and description which enables the route to be followed
without further help, but always take account of the weather and dress accord-
ingly. Remember also that the wind can be very strong at the coast, especially
when you are walking along the cliff-tops! A weather forecast for this area can be
obtained by visiting: www.metoffice.gov.uk or www.bbc.co.uk/weather

The Puffin Shuttle Buses provide an invaluable service, allowing you the lux-
ury of leaving your car behind on your days out (especially if you intend visiting
some of the wonderful pubs!). Details from the transport pages at:
www.pembrokeshire.gov.uk or ring 0871 200 22 33.

Please respect local traditions, and always take special care of the environment, so that all those who wish to share the great charm and beauty of this unique
part of Wales may continue to do so.

Enjoy your walks!

About the author, David Perrott . . .

Having moved with his wife Morag to Machynlleth from London over thirty years
ago, his love of Wales remains as strong now as it was then. He still enjoys walking and cycling in Wales, a part of the British Isles which he believes manages to
combine splendid and varied countryside, and friendly people, within an amazingly
compact area. David & Morag's 'Kittiwake' guides provide an invaluable service for
visitors and residents alike.

CLIMBING TO CEMAES HEAD

DESCRIPTION This 6-mile walk starts at the northern end of the Pembrokeshire Coastal Path, opened by the great Wynford Vaughan Thomas in 1970, and commemorated on a road-side stone here. The path along the top of the cliffs by Cemaes Head is quite spectacular, and the return is made through Cwm yr Esgyr, a remarkably pretty valley.

START Park in the car park at Poppit Sands (charge/café/toilets). Be sure to visit the RNLI shop. SN 152485.

I Leave the car park and walk uphill along the road, with the sea to your right. *The first mile-and-a-half follows the single track road towards Cemaes Head, so forget the tarmac surface and concentrate on the view, especially of Cardigan Island, which may once have been occupied by a Roman marching camp. It became infamous in 1934 when the 6500-ton liner SS Herefordshire ran aground on its north-west corner on the 15 March, where it remained for a few days before sinking into the surrounding waters and disgorging its brown rats onto the island, where they remained until finally being cleared in 1969. Regrettably the rats destroyed the small resident colony of breeding puffins and perhaps also Manx shearwaters. Eight Soay sheep were introduced onto the island in 1944 in order to help to preserve this breed, although it is now thought that the resulting population may currently be doing more harm than good. The island is now notable for its population of fur seals, and is kept as a nature reserve.* After a little over a mile of steady climbing you cross a cattle grid to finally leave the tarmac. Ignore the left-hand fork and continue ahead. When you reach the camp site, do not go uphill by the entrance, but go downhill, turning sharp RIGHT along a track. Passing the camp site to your left, go through the RIGHT-hand gate by a house, continuing through the yard to a small gate. Go through this, then ignore a

path on your left and continue AHEAD. Pass a building on the left and go through a gate up a slope and turn RIGHT along a green track. When you reach a stile on the RIGHT cross it and continue walking, maintaining your direction.

2 Cross a stile beside a gate as the path swings left, then cross another stile and continue. Climb over a stile as you approach the old look-out post then, *trying to be brave, admire the heart-stopping drops to the pebble beach far below and, in the autumn, the seals which frequent these bays.* Continue along the cliff-tops, enjoying the spectacular views, and eventually ignore a stile on the left and continue.

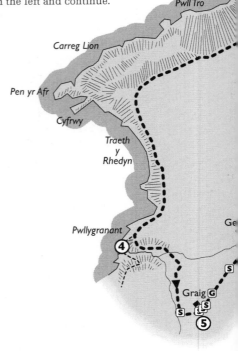

3 Cross a stile into the National Trust property of Pen yr Afr and enjoy a long uninterrupted section until you descend into Pwllygranant, where the path splits by the National Trust sign for Gernos.

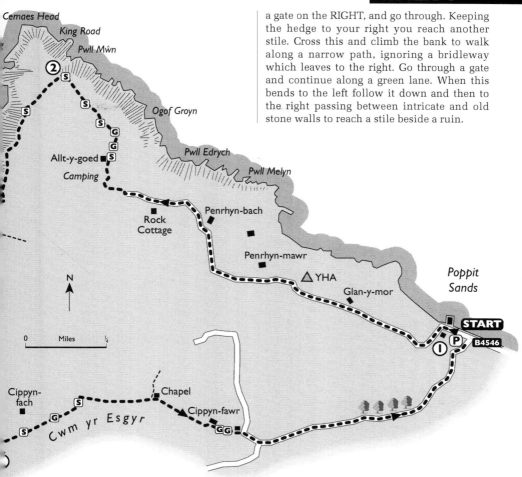

a gate on the RIGHT, and go through. Keeping the hedge to your right you reach another stile. Cross this and climb the bank to walk along a narrow path, ignoring a bridleway which leaves to the right. Go through a gate and continue along a green lane. When this bends to the left follow it down and then to the right passing between intricate and old stone walls to reach a stile beside a ruin.

4 Here you leave the Coastal Path, carrying on ahead and inland. Cross the upper footbridge and continue, climbing steps. At the top of the climb you follow the path to the RIGHT. Descend and ascend steps and continue. You now follow a lovely hollow path to cross a stile and then veer LEFT to walk with a hedge on the left.

5 Cross a stile in the corner to join a track. Turn LEFT, then immediately RIGHT, to cross first one stile, and then another. Cross the track, climb the stile opposite and walk to

6 Cross the stile and turn RIGHT along a farm road. About 40 yards, after passing under electricity cables, cross a stile on the LEFT and follow a lovely green path through woodland. Go through a gate and carry on uphill. Eventually you cross a stile and turn RIGHT. You now walk along an equally fine green track passing a disused chapel by a path junction. Continue ahead, passing Cippyn-fawr and going through two gateways to reach a road. Carry on ahead, then turn LEFT at the junction to return to Poppit Sands.

WALK 2

MOYLGROVE & LLECH Y DRYBEDD

DESCRIPTION This 5-mile walk starts from the pretty, but pub-less, village of Moylgrove. Thanks to the generosity of the nearby Penrallt Ceibwr Garden Centre, you head towards the coast through the wooded Cwm Trewyddel, to emerge at the back of Ceibwr Bay. There then follows a dramatic length of the Coastal Path, passing caves, natural arches and an area of spectacular landslips, some appearing to be surprisingly recent!

Heading inland along the wooded Cwm Ffynnon-alwm, you pass the scant remains of Castelltreruffydd. A very worthwhile diversion of a mile brings you to the sturdy and little visited cromlech of Llech y Drybedd, approached against the backdrop of the prominent summit of Carn Ingli. Your return is along a quiet road, with fine coastal views.

START Park in the car park (toilets [closed in winter]) in the centre of Moylgrove, a village about 4 miles west of Cardigan via St Dogmaels. SN 118447.

1 Leave the car park and turn RIGHT. Walk along the road, keeping left as sign-posted to St Dogmaels, and carry on uphill. When the road swings sharp right and goes steeply uphill, turn LEFT through a wooden gate. You now walk gently downhill through the fine mixed woodland of Cwm Trewyddel. *There are occasional fine views through the trees.* Eventually a path joins from the right, signed to the garden centre – save your visit for later and carry on to eventually join the road at Ceibwr Bay.

2 After crossing the fine clapper bridge to visit the bay, return to the road, turn RIGHT and continue uphill along the road. It's worth making a very short diversion over the grass to your right in order to get a better view of the wonderfully rocky shoreline. Rejoin the road and continue until you reach a sign indicating the Coastal Path to your RIGHT. Follow this, *enjoying views of some spectacular landslips.* You descent to Traeth Bach, crossing over the arch where similar landslips have almost enclosed a tidal pool, known as the Witches Cauldron. Now climb steeply out of the bay by Carrog Yspar to reach two stiles.

3 Cross the LEFT-HAND stile and walk along the path to a second stile by the scant remains of Castelltreruffydd. Cross this and veer left along the narrow path through the woods of Cwm Ffynnon-alwm, where there are further landslips. Climb steps to cross a stile, turn LEFT and continue to a junction, where you turn RIGHT. Walk along a green track to go through a gate to reach a lane. Turn RIGHT here *(the clear track to the left, which would provide the option of a shorter return to Moylgrove, is private for the first 100 yards or so).* Cross a stile and walk to the right of farm buildings. Pass a new house on the right, then turn LEFT around the farm and continue along a track to reach the road by crossing a stile beside a gate.

4 Turn RIGHT and walk along the road (keep children with you in case of traffic) for about 200 yards, then turn LEFT along a concrete track signed to 'Penlan'. Carry on ahead when the concrete track turns to the left. When the track forks go LEFT and carry on, looking out for a stile on the RIGHT giving access to Llech y Drybedd. *This can be viewed against the backdrop of Carn Ingli from where, in legend, St Samson threw it. Hence its other name – Samson's Quoit. It is also known as the Altar Stone, or the Stone of the Three Graves. There may at one time have been a fourth supporting stone.*

5 Now retrace your steps to the road and turn RIGHT to return to Moylgrove, *taking care and looking out for traffic.* There are fine coastal views as you reach the village. *You can visit the nearby Penrallt Ceibwr Garden Centre, where there is an excellent café. It is signed off the road to St Dogmaels.*

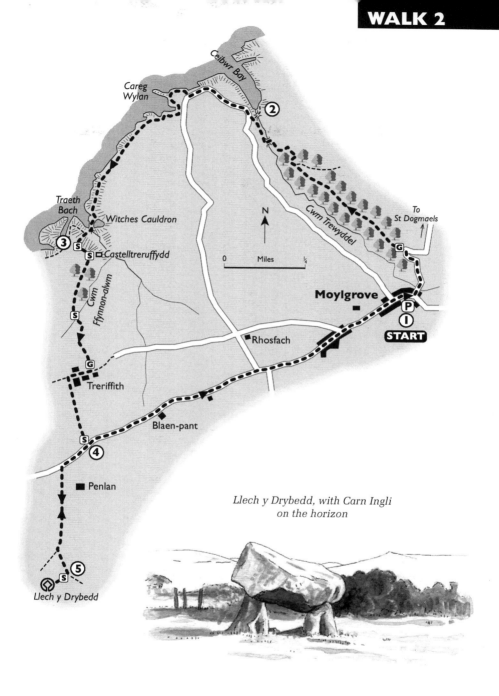

Celbwr Bay

Careg
Wylan

②

Cwm Trewyddel

To
St Dogmaels

Ⓖ

Traeth
Bach

Witches Cauldron

③ Ⓢ
Ⓢ ⊡ Castelltreruffydd

N

0   Miles   ¼

Moylgrove

Ⓖ

Ⓟ
①
START

Ⓢ

Cwm Ffynnon-alwm

■ Rhosfach

Ⓖ
Treriffith

Blaen-pant

Ⓢ
④

■ Penlan

*Llech y Drybedd, with Carn Ingli
on the horizon*

Ⓢ ⑤
◎
Llech y Drybedd

WALK 3

NEWPORT & CARN INGLI

DESCRIPTION Start south of the main road through the town to walk up to Market Street and past the church to soon gain access to Carningli Common. You then walk around the edge of the common to begin a gradual climb through first bracken and then heather brings you to Carn Ingli's summit, where you can enjoy stunning views over the coast and inland. Away from the summit it's an easy descent heading towards Newport and enjoying a wonderful view over the coast and estuary. The summit is rocky and steep, so take great care when you clamber over the stones, and the paths can be confusing, so do NOT venture up in misty conditions, when you cannot see surrounding landmarks. 3 miles, with steep sections.
START Park in the car park (toilets) opposite the Information Centre in Heol Hîr, Newport. SN 059392.

I From the car park turn RIGHT return to the main road, cross it and walk up Market Street. Turn LEFT into Church Street at the top to walk around to the right, passing St Mary's church on your left. *A church was built on this site by the Normans, and dedicated to St Curig. It was rebuilt and rededicated in the 13th century, and the tower survives from this period. The building was enlarged in 1835, and completely restored in 1879.* Pass below the castle to your right, and later a little bakery, where you can buy fresh bread. *Pass by cottages which were the base of Madam Beavan's Circulating School from 1819-70.* Fork RIGHT at College Square to walk along a 'No Through Road'. Continue uphill and at the top turn LEFT as signed

to 'Bryneithen'. Pass a house on the left and continue. At a junction with a narrow tarmac lane turn RIGHT uphill along a track. Pass 'Penfeidr Newydd' on the left and continue to a gate.

2 Go through the gate and carry on AHEAD. A gate in a wall soon appears on the right. Now, do not walk straight ahead but veer RIGHT then turn LEFT up a clear path, counting 100 yards as you walk uphill to a cross-paths, where you turn LEFT. Continue along the path, passing first one track off to the left, and then another. Ignore a faint track off to the right and follow the clear track ahead and slightly downhill. A wall joins from the left.

3 You reach a wide track at a T junction and turn RIGHT, to walk gently uphill with a wall to your left. Pass an opening in the wall to your left and continue. You then reach a junction of five paths. Turn HALF-RIGHT uphill on a clear track and continue.

4 Eventually you join a path which stretches from a car park by the road below to the summit. Turn sharp RIGHT uphill. Now follow the path towards the summit, which zig-zags as it passes heaps of stones. Generally veer left towards the highest summit, and pick your way to the top to enjoy the wonderful views.

5 To return, walk towards the lowest summit, pass to the right of it to pick up a narrow path, which eventually crosses through the remains of a fallen stone wall, and follow the path downhill, always generally in the direction of St Mary's church tower. After passing by an outcrop of rock and a wooden stump, take the left hand path towards the church. Soon you descend fairly steeply to rejoin your outward path, passing the church on the way.

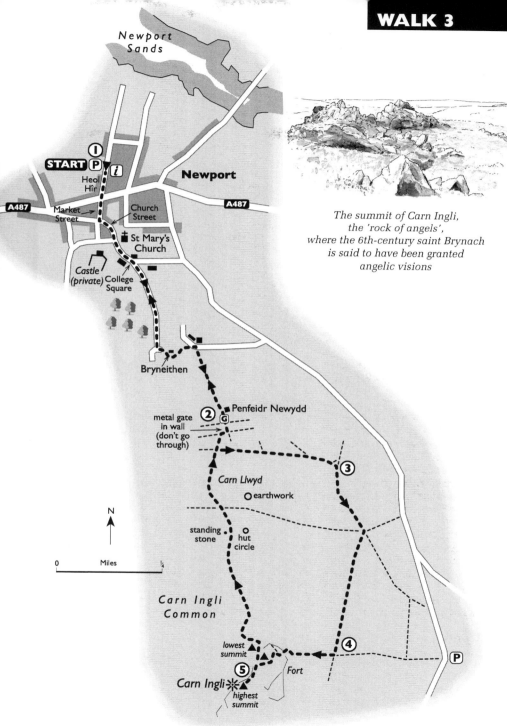

The summit of Carn Ingli,
the 'rock of angels',
where the 6th-century saint Brynach
is said to have been granted
angelic visions

Newport
Sands

START

Newport

Heol
Hîr

A487

A487

Market
Street

Church
Street

St Mary's
Church

Castle
(private)

College
Square

Bryneithen

Penfeidr Newydd

metal gate
in wall
(don't go
through)

Carn Llwyd

earthwork

N

standing
stone

hut
circle

0   Miles   ½

Carn Ingli
Common

lowest
summit

Carn Ingli

Fort

highest
summit

WALK 4

DINAS ISLAND & ABER FOREST

DESCRIPTION A 5-mile route which encircles Dinas Island, giving outstanding views over Fishguard Bay as you climb to the 460-foot high summit You then skirt Newport Bay, again with splendid views, before walking through Cwm-yr-Eglwys, with its ruined church standing right at the sea's edge. Ultimately you turn inland at Aber Fforest to make a very pleasant cross-country return to The Old Sailors pub/restaurant and car park. Dinas Island is not in fact an island — it was formed by the same ice age meltwater that created the Gwaun Valley to the south (see **Walk 6**).

START Leave the A487 just east of Dinas Cross and drive through Bryn-henllan to reach the car park and toilets at Pwllgwaelod. SN 004399.

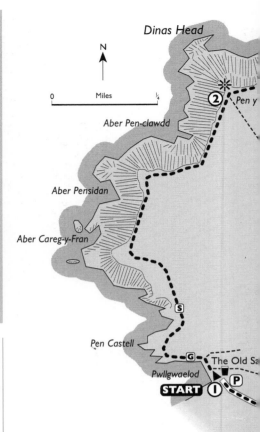

Dinas Head

N

0   Miles   ¼

Aber Pen-clawdd

Aber Pensidan

Aber Careg-y-Fran

Pen Castell

Pwllgwaelod

Pen y

The Old Sa

START

Leave the car park and with the sea to your left walk up the concrete track towards Island Farm and, when the track swings right, continue ahead through a gate to walk along the Coastal Path. Soon you start climbing. When the path splits take the RIGHT hand route away from the crumbling cliff edge. Cross a stile and continue, enjoying a fine view over the bay towards Fishguard. Continue, to reach the trig point at the summit of Pen y Fan. *This windswept headland and the adjacent cliffs are typically covered with bracken, bramble, gorse, stunted hawthorn, hazel and blackthorn, and small ash and oak trees where a little shelter can be found. Spring brings a flush of bluebells, and you should also look out for heather, ling, thrift, pennywort, foxgloves and the odd orchid.*

2 Continue along the path, ignoring a stile on the right which leads towards Island Farm. You start gradually descending, now enjoying a fine view of Newport. Go through-kissing-gates and, after a short distance, the path forks. Go LEFT and start to descend, then climb and go through another kissing-

gate. *The area around Needle Rock is an excellent place to watch sea-birds — in the summer you might see fulmars, guillimots, razorbills and shag, while in winter chough, a variety of gulls and ravens will be seen. Inland you might find stonechats and warblers.* Continue, crossing a stile and descending steeply down steps. Maintain your direction when a path joins from the right.

3 Go through a kissing-gate to leave National Trust property. Descend steeply down the path and steps. Cross a bridge and turn LEFT to reach Cwm-yr-Eglwys. *Visit the remains of the 12th century St Brynach's church, which stand at the water's edge. Part of this building was swept away in the 'Royal Charter' storm of October 1859, during a*

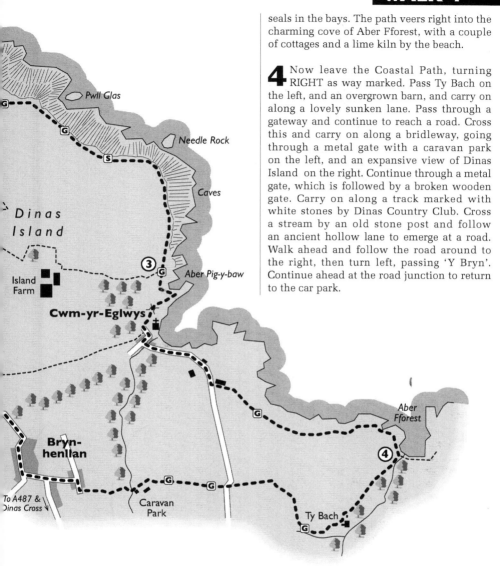

seals in the bays. The path veers right into the charming cove of Aber Fforest, with a couple of cottages and a lime kiln by the beach.

4 Now leave the Coastal Path, turning RIGHT as way marked. Pass Ty Bach on the left, and an overgrown barn, and carry on along a lovely sunken lane. Pass through a gateway and continue to reach a road. Cross this and carry on along a bridleway, going through a metal gate with a caravan park on the left, and an expansive view of Dinas Island on the right. Continue through a metal gate, which is followed by a broken wooden gate. Carry on along a track marked with white stones by Dinas Country Club. Cross a stream by an old stone post and follow an ancient hollow lane to emerge at a road. Walk ahead and follow the road around to the right, then turn left, passing 'Y Bryn'. Continue ahead at the road junction to return to the car park.

two-week period which claimed 748 lives and 325 shipwrecks around the British Isles. Join a road and turn LEFT by 'Tides Reach', and walk beside vines and subtropical vegetation. Turn LEFT along a lane by 'Parc Penrhiw'. Go through a gate and continue along a narrow path – when it splits you can take either route. There are fine views, and you may see

The Old Sailors Pwllgwaelod, Bryn-henllan. 01348 811491. Tiny bar offering real ale, restaurant serving good food (including scallops), and friendly staff. Pleasant garden overlooking Fishguard Bay, where, if you are fortunate, you can watch the porpoises.

LLANWNDA
et quelques visiteurs Français

DESCRIPTION A 4-mile walk which dips into a fascinating historical event – the last invasion of Britain – and starts by a very pretty little church which was at one time part of the estate of Pebidiog. The countryside and coast here is wonderfully remote, although it is just a mile from Fishguard. Try to visit The Royal Oak in the town, to put a fitting end to your walk, and the story.

START Park by church in Llanwnda. SM 932396.

St Gwyndaf's is a small late-medieval church which stands on the site of an earlier building. When it was undergoing restoration in 1881 seven early Christian monuments were revealed, dating from the 7th–11th centuries, decorated with a hooded monk, a cleric and crosses. Five can be seen in the outside wall, with another, a decorated cross base, lying in undergrowth to the north-west. The church stands in the ancient area of the episcopal lordship of Pebidiog, and the parish was an important prebend of St David's (ie it paid a stipend to the cathedral). In legend St Gwyndaf cursed the stream here, leaving it without fish, after breaking his leg following an argument with St Aidan. Take the 'Road Unsuitable for Motors' opposite the church. When the road splits either side of a gate, go the the RIGHT along a lovely hollow lane, which was at one time a surfaced road. *About half way along this lane you cross Pont Eglwys, which may have marked the boundary of an early ecclesiastical estate, possibly an an important centre in pre-Conquest Wales.* When you reach a road turn RIGHT and then immediately RIGHT again towards Castell, following a concrete track. Follow this track around the house and continue to a T junction. *The farm buildings here are Tre-Howel, which were used as French headquarters during the invasion of 1797 (see 3 below).*

2 Turn RIGHT through a gate and continue along the track, with a sea view ahead. When you reach a track junction, go to the RIGHT and continue. Stay on the track when it swings to the right. Swing right again to reach a stile between gates. Cross it and continue to reach two gates with a stile to the left. Cross this and carry on ahead until a waymark post directs you to veer HALF-LEFT along a rough, narrow, path.

3 You join the Coastal Path at a stile on your left. Cross this to visit Carregwastad Point and the memorial stone to the French 'invasion'. *This took place on 22nd February 1797, and is a tale worthy of the Marx Brothers. A French fleet, carrying 1000 soldiers, had planned to land in Ireland to pick up more rebels, but was blown off course during a gale and opted to land at Fishguard. However, worried about the presence of the fort, built after an earlier French raid in 1776, they chose Carregwasted Point as the place to start their invasion. It was a poor choice, and the Frenchmen were soon demoralised and rounded up by pitchfork carrying locals, known as the Fishguard Fencibles. One women, Jemima Nicholas, rounded up 14 soldiers by herself, and took them to Fishguard jail. A memorial in the wall of St Mary's church, Fishguard, commemorates this brave 47-year-old woman. The surrender treaty was signed in The Royal Oak pub, in Market Square, Fishguard, where the table used can still be seen. This event is also comemorated in the Fishguard tapestry, which can be seen in the Town Hall nearby. The town is also notable as the being the home town of Black Bart, who is credited with the invention of the Jolly Roger's skull and crossbones. His head was shot off by a canon ball in 1722.* Return to the stile, cross it and turn LEFT to follow the Coastal Path.

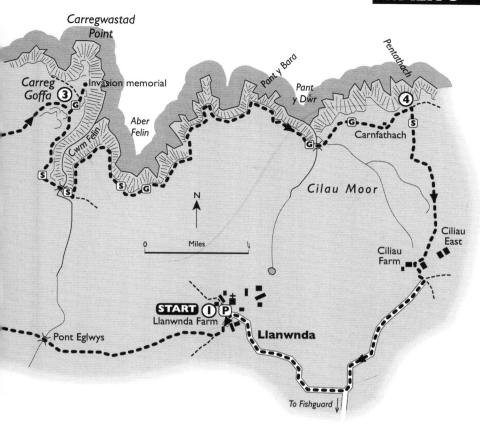

You now continue along the path over stiles and through gates as it heads east towards Carnfathach, constantly dipping and climbing, often quite steeply. *Look out for seals at Aberfelin and in the subsequent bay.*

4 When the long low spit of Pentathach appears below, turn RIGHT as signed, leaving the Coastal Path and heading inland with a wall on your left. Cross a stile and continue, using stepping stones to cross a marshy patch. Turn LEFT at a path junction and follow a grassy track towards Cilau Farm. Turn RIGHT as waymarked. Veer RIGHT at the farm and turn RIGHT as signed. Now continue along the lane, turning RIGHT when signed to Llanwnda, to return to your car.

If you can, finish your outing by travelling to Fishguard, to visit **The Royal Oak** *pub,* *where you can enjoy a pint of real ale, some decent pub food and probably a chat with the locals. At the rear of the bar you will see the table on which the aforementioned peace treaty was signed.*

The Royal Oak
Market Square, Fishguard, SA65 9HA.
01348 872514.

WALK 6
CWM GWAUN
& BESSIE'S PUB

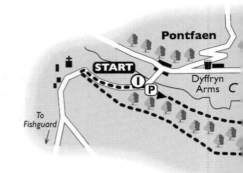

DESCRIPTION Cwm Gwaun is a relic of the last Ice Age, formed by huge volumes of water flowing under the ice from melting glaciers. Today it is a very peaceful and thickly wooded valley, rich with oak and beech, its water meadows scattered with bluebells in Spring. Wood and willow warblers can be seen in summer, while kingfishers, grey wagtails and dippers may be seen darting around by the stream. There is also a population of Dormice. The road, quiet now, was once the main turnpike road from Haverfordwest to Newport. Indeed the valley is a remarkable survival of quieter times, where the local people refused to accept the 18th century modernisation of the calendar, and celebrated New Year, Hen Galan, on January 13th. This easy 3-mile walk expores the woods opposite Pontfaen and gives a view of Dwfr Ddisgynfa Cwm-du waterfalls, tucked down in the cwm. Seemingly as ancient as the woods is Bessie Davies' pub, the Dyffryn Arms. A remarkable survivor where you can enjoy a pint of real ale straight from the barrel, and a friendly chat.

START The car park is on the right-hand side about 50 yards beyond Cwm Gwaun, marked by a stone, as you approach Pontfaen from the B4313. Stout footwear is needed. SN 025340.

1 Take the obvious path from the car park along the edge of the woods. Ignore a path which comes in from the right (or take it IF you want a VERY short walk!) and continue through Pontfaen Woods.

2 When you reach a path junction (where you can turn right for the second shorter alternative) continue ahead and downhill, swinging left around farm buildings. DON'T cross the stile ahead, but turn RIGHT to cross a footbridge beside a ford and follow the lane, turning RIGHT along a bridle way and ignoring a gate and stile ahead. The track climbs steadily. Ignore a lesser track which forks to the right and carry on uphill. The path climbs and bends left through a muddy patch as you reach a sign post.

3 Turn RIGHT and follow the path down steps towards the Afon Cwmau, tumbling down the cwm to join the Afon Gwaun in the valley below. Cross a footbridge, climb steps and turn RIGHT. Carry on through trees, with waterfalls to the right and the occasional view across the valley through breaks in the trees. Pass the way mark post indicating one of the aforementioned shorter alternative routes and continue ahead. Pass the second 'short walk' path on the right and continue to the road. Turn RIGHT to return to the car park, or turn left to visit the tiny church of St Brynach. *Brynach came to Wales from Ireland in the 6th century. He landed at what is now Milford Haven and was picked upon for resisting the advances of a local nobleman's daughter. He then moved to the Gwaun Valley, where he drove away evil spirits whose howling had made the valley uninhabitable. Have a look in the graveyard for two tall stones. Although carved in the 9th century with crosses, their origin may be pre-Christian. And don't forget to visit the* **Dyffryn Arms** *– plain, simple and unique.*

Over the hill to the west are the remains of what was once Europe's largest ammunition store. The 1000-acre site, with 58 bomb-proof tunnels and its own railway system, was closed in 1995, with a subsequent loss of local jobs.

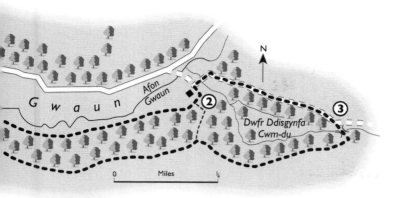

Bessie's pub

PORTHGAIN HARBOUR

DESCRIPTION A stunning 3½-mile walk from the old industrial village of Porthgain, which includes a quiet valley falling towards the little seaside village of Abereiddy. On the headland you can visit the Blue Lagoon before returning along the Pembrokeshire Coastal Path passing a series of rocky bays and headlands before reaching the mellow quarry remains of Porthgain. Finally you can reward your modest efforts with a pint at the Sloop, a fine old inn.

START Park in the car park area in Porthgain, which is north-west of Croes-goch on the A487. SM 815326.

I Walk back inland along the minor road and fork RIGHT down the lane signed to Ynys Barry Holiday Cottages, veering RIGHT along the tarmac lane. Continue ahead between two squat white gateposts with a wrought-iron gate to walk through the farmyard, by-passing a gate and ten going through a gate to leave the yard. Carry on along the track, passing through a gateway and enjoying fine sea views to the north, with Carn Llidi and Carn Perfedd in the south-west.

2 Reach a sign post by a gate and a stile. Cross the stile and turn LEFT, to walk with a fence and bank on your left. Carry on ahead when the fence veers away from your route. Reach a stile, cross it and veer right to walk towards Abereiddy, gradually descending.

3 As you approach an overgrown gate ahead, turn left down a narrow path towards a gate beside a little toilet block. Go through the gate and turn RIGHT towards the 'Gents', then LEFT through a second gate. After a short distance turn RIGHT along a clear concrete path uphill. Veer off LEFT of this to visit the Blue Lagoon. *This flooded slate quarry is about 100-feet deep, and is the result of serious production which began here in the 1840s. By 1848 a steam engine had been installed to service the various galleries, and by 1851 sixteen quarry men were working here. At that time there were no railways in Pembrokeshire, and as there was no proper harbour here, slate was exported using sloops which were beached at high tide. This system could only operate during the summer months and the maximum cargo was a modest 30 tons. With no possibility of building a harbour at Abereiddy, it was decided to utilise Porthgain, where there was good shelter, and link them with a tramway. Construction was put in hand in 1851.*

Cerrig Gwylan

4 Now return to the junction with the Coastal Path and turn LEFT, climbing to get a good view over the Blue Lagoon and continuing, with the sea to your left. Go through a kissing-gate and carry on, soon passing steps down to the beach at Traeth Llyfn. Walk above Porth Egr, an inaccessible inlet favoured by seals, and carry on. As you approach Porthgain you walk beside an old tramway cutting, with ruined buildings beyond. *A cave extends into the headland at sea level.* You then pass through a kissing-gate and descend stone steps to the handsome industrial harbour of Porthgain. *Construction of the harbour began in earnest in 1851, and a quarry was opened just 150 yards from the quays, financed by the Barry Island Slate and Slab Company. Houses for the workers were erected at Porthgain Row and Pentop Terrace, with various larger houses for the management. Initially the quarry worked well, but as the pit became deeper, the problems of lifting material over the rim and then back down to the harbour increased. Water also had to be pumped from the workings, and all of this was executed using horse power alone. The company was declared bankrupt in 1860 and*

Carn Lŵyd

Blue Lagoon

course of tram

toilets

Abereiddi Bay

Abereidd

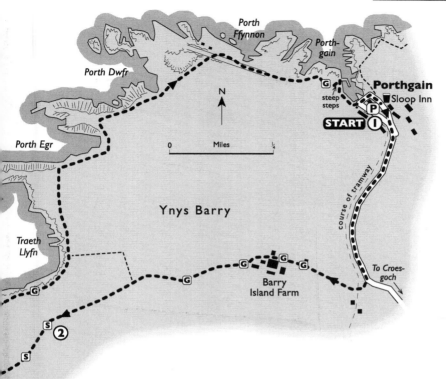

was put up for sale. It changed hands several times before the turn of the century, often with periods of inactivity and rarely generating any real income. Fortunes began changing in the early 1900s with the construction of a brickworks, and the discovery of blue and green slate, and very fine granite (strictly speaking 'andesite') close by. A tunnel was constructed to connect the quarry to the mills and the wharf, and a machine house by the harbour processed the material. Storage bins on the quay side and more steam engines, stationery and mobile, were installed, and by 1910 the scene was set for Porthgain's most prosperous period of operation. The company owned three steamers, and supplied over seventy local councils with roadstone, and soon this was the only material being supplied. Being wholly dependent upon the sea to transport its granite, the submarine activity of the Great War had a

disastrous effect upon trade, and the quarry ran down and became neglected. Attempts were made to revive the plant after the war, but production never equalled pre-war levels. As road-building methods changed demand dropped until, on 23rd July 1931, production ended. Remaining stocks and waste material were cleared over the next couple of years and the industry never returned. It now remains a fascinating testament to the type of small-scale endeavour that once thrived around the coast of Britain before the coming of road transport. Walk by the harbour to return to the car park.

The Sloop Inn has borne witness to the last couple of hundred years of history of this little harbour, and now thrives thanks to those walking the Pembrokeshire Coastal Path, or spending their holidays in the area. They serve real ale along with excellent food, and the pub is friendly and welcoming. Outdoor seating.

WALK 8
WHITESANDS BAY & CARN LLIDI

DESCRIPTION A 4-mile walk from the northern end of Whitesands Bay passing two wonderful sandy coves, before heading out to the westerly tip of St David's Head for stunning views of Ramsey Island down to the south. The northern coastal section is wonderfully rough and craggy, with the path crossing short coastal grassland before turning inland to climb around Carn Llidi and then striking out for the summit. From here you will be able to survey the whole of your route, before you return to the start via the handsome farm of Upper Porthmawr.

START Start from the car park (charge) at Whitesands Bay, at the end of the B4583 north-west of St David's. SM 734272.

1 From the car park follow the Coastal Path north, with the sea to your left. *You can make a diversion around the headland of Trwynhwrddyn if you wish.* Continue along the Coastal Path, gently climbing around Porth Lleuog to soon reach the gate which takes you onto National Trust Land. *You have a fine view of Ramsey Island, with Careg Rhoson and North Bishop to its west.*

2 Go through the gate and continue along the path, passing around the sandy cove of Porthmelgan and out onto the headland. Here you can leave the Coastal Path and continue further west to walk around St David's Head, crossing the remains of an ancient embankment, once part of a fortification. *About 100 yards from these remains stands Coetan Arthur, probably a collapsed dolmen some 4000 years old, with a capstone which, when seen from a certain angle, seems to mimic the profile of Carn Llidi. Keep a sharp look-out for this, as it can be easily missed. There is a rough path from the Coastal Path which will take you up to the site. This area was once a settlement of the Iron Age*

Demetae folk. Pick your way through the rocks and heather to rejoin the Coastal Path, and continue. Eventually you descend to a sign posted path junction, with a stone wall ahead and to your right.

3 At the path junction (where the signpost may well have fallen over), turn right as directed towards the Youth Hostel. Continue along the grassy path, which soon bends left towards an old stone wall, then turns right to begin climbing the hill ahead, with the wall to your left. Now just follow the path over the brow, veering right and descending with the wall. Pass the gate on the left which gives access to the Youth Hostel and continue.

4 Descend to a track at a T junction, and remember this point – you will return here. Ahead there is a fine view over Whitesands Bay. Turn RIGHT and, after a short while fork RIGHT, by a National Trust stone sign, up a clear track towards the summit of Carn Llidi Bychan. *Carn Llidi is a well-hidden double-chambered tomb overlooking a Neolithic field system. Sir Richard Cold Hoare wrote of this area in his Journal of a Tour of Wales 1793: 'No place could ever be more suited to retirement, contemplation or Druidical mysteries, surrounded by inaccessible rock and open to a wide expanse of ocean. Nothing seems wanting but the thick impenetrable groves of oaks which have been thought concomitant to places of Druidical worship and which, from the exposed nature of this situation, would never, I think, have existed here even in former days'.* Pass between two rusting metal posts and carry on up an old concrete path to reach the foundations of an old defensive installation. *This was used as a hydrophone station, for detecting submarines, in World War I, and a radar station in World War II.* From here you can follow a rough path to the summit if you wish, to survey the whole of your route.

16

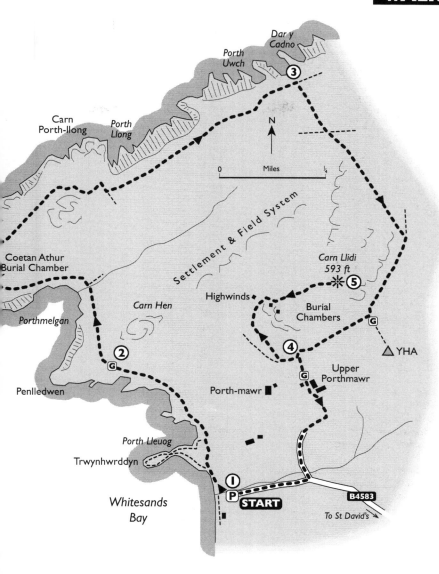

5 Return down the path to the junction at point **4** and carry on ahead to cross a stile beside a metal gate. Pass between the attractive and traditional farm buildings of Upper Porthmawr. Veer RIGHT along the track *and take a look back at this wonder-* *fully unspoiled farmhouse.* Descend along the track which bends right, then left, to join a road, all the while enjoying the views. Turn RIGHT at the road to return to the car park, where there are toilets and a summer café and gift shop.

ST DAVID'S & ST NON'S

DESCRIPTION Allow yourself plenty of time for this 3½-mile walk, since there is so much to see. It is probably a good idea to visit the Cathedral and Bishop's Palace when you have completed the circuit, so that you can spend the maximum amout of time there. Meanwhile you will have plenty to see and enjoy on the route, including St Non's Chapel and Well, an excellent stretch of coast, a narrow sheltered harbour where you can get a cup of tea, and an easy return with a fine view of the Cathedral.

START The Cathedral car park, St David's (modest charge). SM 749253.

I From the car park return to the road and turn RIGHT, passing the Cathedral to your left. Continue along Goat Street until you reach Stephen's Lane on your right. Walk down Stephen's Lane and turn LEFT at the end. Take the first RIGHT by the Bryn y Garn sign and continue to the end. Turn right to walk along a track for a short distance, then turn LEFT along a path signed for St Nons.

2 Cross a stile and continue with the field edge on your left. Turn RIGHT at the field corner, then shortly turn LEFT through a gap and walk with the field edge on your left to reach a stile. Cross it, turn RIGHT and cross another stile (*there may be an electric fence on this field – take care*), then turn LEFT over the next stile. Carry on AHEAD to cross a stile and then follow the path as it swings down and zig-zags to meet the coastal path.

3 Turn RIGHT and take the RIGHT HAND of two paths to pass St Non's Retreat and the new Chapel of Our Lady & St Non. *This chapel was built in 1934 in the native style (which was used around 500AD), using many stones reclaimed from other early religious buildings in the area. The stained glass window shows Saints Bride, Brynach, David and Winifred. A white heart-shaped stone in the chapel originated from the altar of St Patrick's Chapel, and many of the incised stones came from the altar of St Non's Chapel. The retreat is a place of calm and pilgrimmage for the local Welsh community.* Pass through a gate to reach St Non's Well. *This is one of Wales' most sacred wells, which sprang up during a thunderstorm upon the birth of St David. The waters are said to have miraculaous healing qualities. In 1717 it was described in a Survey of St David's: 'There is a fine Well beside it (St. Non's Chapel), cover'd with a Stone-Roof, and enclos'd within a Wall, with Benches to sit upon round the Well. People still visit, especially upon St. Nun's Day (March 2nd), 'which they kept holy, and offer Pins, Pebbles, Ec at this well'.* Pass through a kissing gate to reach the remains of St Non's Chapel. *St Non was the mother of St David – this is said to mark his place of birth. It contains a 9th-century creed stone inscribed with a Latin ring cross.* Continue on the grassy path to cross a stile and join the Pembrokeshire Coast National Trail. Turn RIGHT. Now continue along the coastal path to pass Porth Ffynnon before reaching Porth Clais – *a deep inlet popular with rock climbers and canoeists, and which was once the main port for St David's where corn, malt, wool, limestone and timber were shipped. In legend the giant boar Twrch Trwyth came ashore here, pursued by King Arthur.* You pass above the harbour breakwater and eventually the path splits. Go LEFT to reach the lime kilns, toilets and a very handy summer tea kiosk.

4 Now, with the sea to your right, pass wooden gates and take the signed path which leaves the road and climbs. Pass through a gate to cross a field which is also a camping site. Turn LEFT just before the house and then turn RIGHT through a gate to follow a fenced path. Go through four more gates, and then the path bears right to reach a road.

5 Cross the road and go along the track opposite for about 15 yards, then turn LEFT. When you reach Mitre Lane continue AHEAD. You then join your outward route where you turn LEFT to return to the car park. *However, **The Farmers Arms** is well worth visiting, with real ale, food and a garden, and if you turn right beside it you will reach the Cathedral and the Bishop's Palace. A monastery was founded by St David on the current cathedral site in 589 AD, and was attacked, destroyed and rebuilt many times between 645-1097, until it became a centre of pilgrimmage in 1123. The present building was begun in 1181, and in spite of the tower collapsing in 1220, and the building being damaged in an earthquake 1247-48 it was eventually completed. In 1648 the Parliamentarians destroyed the Cathedral, but rebuilding by Nash was started in 1793 and was completed by Sir George Gilbert Scott 1862-77. The Bishop's Palace, even in its semi-ruined state, remains a very impressive building. It was once the home of the Bishops of St David's, who were prosperous and built this splendid edifice in the 13th and 14th centuries. It fell into disuse and decay during the 16th and 17th centuries. There is a very fine gift shop.*

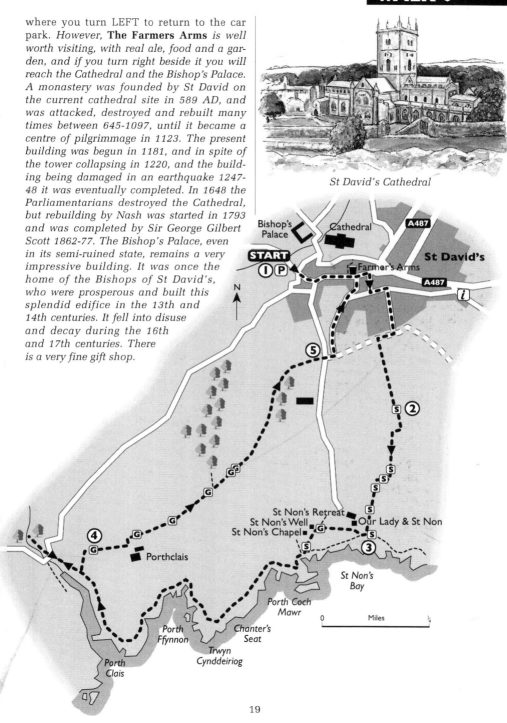

St David's Cathedral

19

SOLVA & ST ELVIS' CROMLECH

DESCRIPTION A very scenic 2-mile walk, which can be extended by walking out to Dinas Fawr (but see the warning in instruction **5**). Initially you will climb above the beautiful harbour for stunning views, before heading inland, crossing a verdant marshy valley to reach St Elvis' cromlech. Then it is out to the coast for a cliff-top return and a walk back to the pub by the water's edge.

START Park in the car park by the Harbour Inn, Solva. SM 806243

1 Cross the bridge by the inn, turn LEFT and then very soon RIGHT to walk up the well hidden Coastal Path. When the path splits, go LEFT through a gate and carry on climbing.

2 When you join a path at the top, turn LEFT. *There are very fine views from here. Solva harbour is a very fine example of a 'ria' – a channel formed by meltwater at the end of the last ice age. If you have an interest in fossils, it is apparently a good place to look for examples from the Cambrian era. It developed from a small natural harbour into the major trading port for the St Bride's area – in Victorian times there were 10 working lime-kilns, and you will pass the remains of some of these later on the walk. It is a very safe anchorage on what can be quite an exposed length of coast.* Follow the clear path along the ridge to a gate and go through. Fork RIGHT through a second gate and turn RIGHT to descend the hillside. Ignore a path which joins from the left then, when the path splits, go RIGHT downhill to a stile. Cross it to walk beside verdant marshland, rich with irises.

3 You come to a bridge with lifting stiles. Cross it, veer RIGHT then LEFT to climb through woods. Cross a stile and carry on ahead to a gate. Cross another stile and continue ahead to a gate. Go through and soon climb steps up to a kissing-gate. Go through. Continue ahead to cross first one stile, then another, and turn LEFT along a track. *At certain times of year there may be young cattle here. Speak to them nicely but firmly and they should move out of your way!*

4 Continue along the track, crossing a stile to reach stones built as a cromlech, in a gated enclosure. *These are the remains of a neolithic burial chamber built about 5000 years ago. Hidden by the nearby farm buildings is the site of St Teilo's church. Teilo was a friend of St David, and accompanied him on a journey to Jerusalem. The font and the cross from this church can be seen in the church in Solva. St Elvis was St David's religious teacher.* Cross the stile ahead, turn RIGHT and cross a second stile and continue ahead along a wide track, crossing two stiles and passing through a gate to reach the car park.

5 Here you can, if you wish, divert to visit the dramatic and heather clad peninsula of Dinas Fawr – there is a right of way out to the point – *if you dare!* **(and you have been warned**: it is very precipitous and UNSUITABLE for very young children and those who are not sure-footed). Otherwise turn RIGHT over the stile and continue along the Coastal Path, high on the cliffs and overlooking a series of bays. You cross two stiles, go through a gate and cross another stile before arriving above Gwadn bay and St Elvis' Rock. Swing right to descend to the beach of this beautiful bay, crossing a bank of stones to reach a footbridge.

6 Cross the footbridge, go through a gate and climb steeply to cross the scant remains of an ancient embanked settlement. Swing right to descend to lime kilns by the water's edge *(if you are with children* **BEWARE** *– one kiln is open at the top).* The path then splits – you can return along the beach at low water, or take the Coastal Path if you wish. **The Harbour Inn** *at Solva is beautifully situated, and you can reward yourself with a pint! The view along the harbour from here is wonderful, with lots of moored craft of all shapes and sizes.*

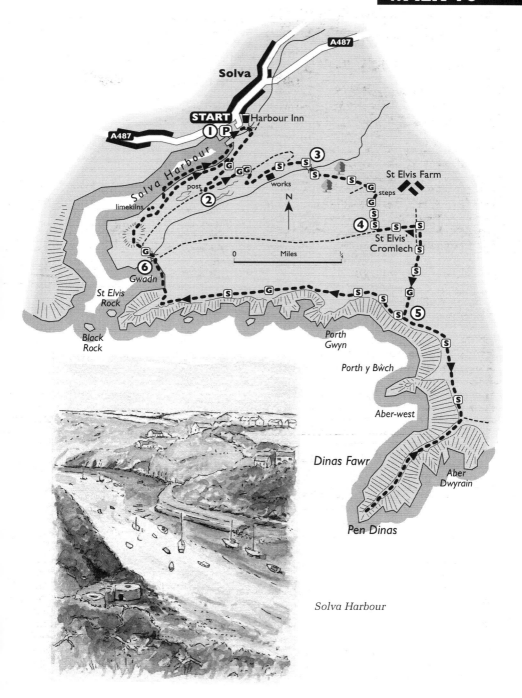

Solva Harbour

21

WALK 11

MARLOES & MARTIN'S HAVEN

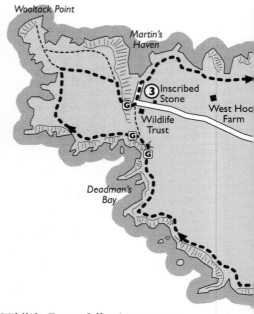

DESCRIPTION A 7-mile walk which is never particularly strenuous but always very rewarding, offering wonderful views of three Pembrokeshire Islands – Gateholm, Skokholm and Skomer – along with the windswept headland of Wooltack Point. Martin's Haven is a departure point for boat trips to the islands, as well as being a very popular venue for scuba divers, who fill this little cove on most summer weekends. They will mostly be crossing the strong tides in Jack Sound to experience the beautiful underwater world of the Skomer Marine Reserve. You can then enjoy a breezy walk along modest cliffs back to Musselwick Sands where you turn back inland to Marloes, and a pint at the Lobster Pot.

START Park outside the Lobster Pot Inn (not in the pub car park), Marloes. SM 792085.

1 With your back to the pub, turn LEFT and walk along the road. Just after the last house on the left, cross a stile on the LEFT and walk with the hedge on your left. When you reach two stiles, cross them, join a lane and turn RIGHT. Walk along the lane for about ¼ mile, then turn LEFT along a track. You pass Green Mire Cottage and the track descends towards Marloes sands.

2 Just above the sands you join the Coastal Path and turn RIGHT, to walk with the sea to your left. Continue, passing Gateholm Island – *which has Romano-British remains and a round barrow* – with Skokholm Island beyond. *Skokholm is a Norse name, meaning 'wooded island'. It became famous due to the work of the naturalist Ronald M Lockley, who leased the island in 1927 and established the first British bird observatory there in 1933. The island had been owned by the Phillips family for 360 years since 1646. With the death of the desecedant Mrs Ostra Lloyd-Phillips in 2005 it was purchased by The*

Wildlife Trusts following a great fund-raising effort. As well as being a base for breeding seabirds, it is also an important site for passage migrants, and many rarities have been seen over the years. The lighthouse was built in 1916, using a donkey-hauled narrow guage railway which ran from the jetty to the site a mile away. The light is 54 metres above mean high water, and has a range of 15 nautical miles. It was automated in 1983. Continue along the path, eventually going through a gate and crossing a footbridge. You can continue directly to Martin's Haven, or take a very worthwhile diversion through the gate and around the headland. *Here you can enjoy views of the islands, see the ponies and have a look at the now defunct Coastguard Look-out Station.* You rejoin the coastal path through a gate and turn LEFT.

3 At Martin's Haven there are handy toilets, an inscribed stone set in the wall beside and a Wildlife Trust shop opposite. Boat trips leave from here to visit Skomer Island, and it is also very popular with scuba divers. The narrow road descends to the

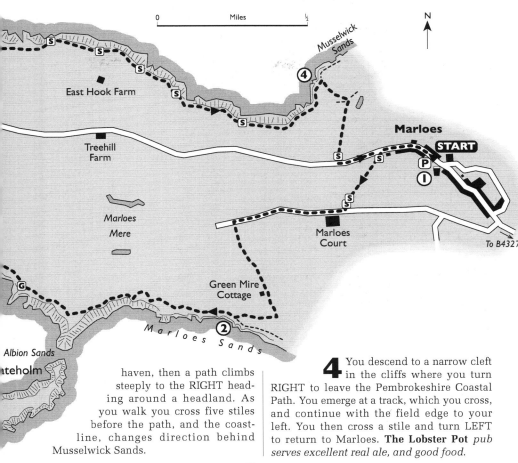

Miles   0 ——————— ½

N ↑

Musselwick Sands

East Hook Farm

Treehill Farm

Marloes

START

P

i

To B4327

Marloes Mere

Marloes Court

Green Mire Cottage

Marloes Sands

Albion Sands

teholm

haven, then a path climbs steeply to the RIGHT heading around a headland. As you walk you cross five stiles before the path, and the coastline, changes direction behind Musselwick Sands.

4 You descend to a narrow cleft in the cliffs where you turn RIGHT to leave the Pembrokeshire Coastal Path. You emerge at a track, which you cross, and continue with the field edge to your left. You then cross a stile and turn LEFT to return to Marloes. **The Lobster Pot** *pub serves excellent real ale, and good food.*

Skomer

WALK 12

DALE & WEST BLOCKHOUSE POINT

DESCRIPTION This 4-mile walk starts from the seashore at Dale, a very popular watersports venue, crowded with windsurfers, sailors and divers during the summer months. From here you walk south across country enjoying sea views to the west and especially the east. Eventually you join the Pembrokeshire Coastal Path near West Blockhouse Point to start your return, all the while overlooking the entrance to Milford Haven, so keep a look out for the variety of ships which use this passage. Finally you join the road giving access to Dale Fort, for an easy return. You can reward yourself in the Griffin Inn, a fine pub.

START The car park at Dale. SM 811059.

I Walk from the car park in Dale with the sea to your left, along the lane and past the Griffin Inn. *Dale was the port where Henry Tudor landed in 1485 on his return from exile in France. His defeat to Richard III at Bosworth Field followed. The port was also a prosperous trading centre.* After passing the last building on your left, a waymark post directs you to steps up the bank on your RIGHT. Climb these, cross a stile and continue with the hedge to your left. Go through a gate and carry on ahead. Go through another gate and keep to the left-hand side of the field, turning RIGHT when you reach trees at the bottom. Walk above a lake to your left, cross two stiles and carry on, keeping the field edge to your left. Continue beyond the end of the lake, then cross a stile on your LEFT and maintain your direction along a track.

2 Leave the farm entrance and turn LEFT to walk along a narrow road. Soon you will enjoy a splendid view to your left over Milford Haven. When the lane doglegs note a stile to your left, which leads directly to Watwick Bay.

3 When the road turns to the left, go through the gate AHEAD and walk down the field, veering slightly to the RIGHT to reach a stile on the Pembrokeshire Coast Path. Cross this and turn LEFT, to walk with the sea to your right. *You are now overlooking the site of one of Britain's most recent maritime disasters, when the oil tanker Sea Empress ran aground at the entrance to Milford Haven, eventually spilling 73,000 tonnes of its 130,000 tonne cargo of North Sea crude oil, a quantity which, in volume, was between that of the Exxon Valdez and the Torrey Canyon. It began on the evening of 15th February 1996 and continued for several days as attempts were made to mitigate the disaster. Eventually the ship was freed and berthed in the Haven, but not before massive environmental and aesthetic damage had been caused. The clean up took about five years, and was hugely expensive, – it cost £28 million – even though only 5300 tonnes of the light crude came ashore. Although the Exxon Valdez was an old style single-hulled design, it was repaired and continued to operate, under another name, until 2004.* Cross a stile and continue around West Blockhouse Point, passing tall navigational beacons, old gun emplacements and the fort. Cross another stile, and then another, to reach the junction mentioned at the end of walk instruction **2**.

4 When you reach a stile, cross it and turn right to follow the clear coastal path over two more stiles before reaching Watwick Point, where there is another navigational beacon, and then another three stiles to reach the back of Castlebeach Bay. Here you cross a footbridge and continue along the path, crossing two more stiles before reaching the road to Dale Fort Field Centre. *Dale Fort has been continuously occupied since Elizabethan times, being substantially rebuilt in the 1850s to protect Milford Haven from the French. In the 1890s it was used for trials of Edmund Zalinski's Pneumatic Dynamite Gun, which used compressed air at 2500 psi, produced by a steam driven compressor, to fire an explosive charge. Unfortunately the guns, the boiler and the compressor weighed in at about 200 tons, so*

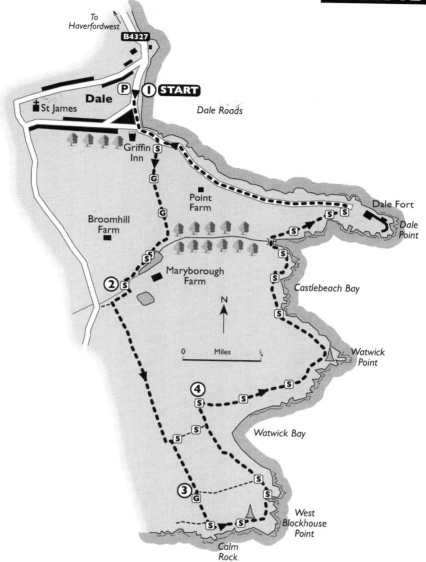

To Haverfordwest
B4327
P START
Dale
St James
Dale Roads
Griffin Inn
G
Point Farm
G
Broomhill Farm
Maryborough Farm
N
2
0 Miles ¼
Dale Fort
Dale Point
Castlebeach Bay
Watwick Point
Watwick Bay
4
3
G
West Blockhouse Point
Calm Rock

the idea was dropped. Since 1947 it has been owned by the Field Studies Council, and is used by thousands of students each year, who study mainly marine biology, ecology, geology and geomorphology. The fort is reputedly haunted, with strange glowing apparitions being seen in the corridors during the early hours, accompanied by a drop in the ambi-

ent temperature. Turn LEFT to return to the start. **The Griffin Inn**, *Dale, is a popular watering hole for the watersports enthusiasts and students from the field centre, where you can enjoy real ale and good food in very welcoming surroundings. Sublime in summer, the front of the building has been lashed by waves during winter storms.*

A DIFFERENT ANGLE

DESCRIPTION It's easy to associate Milford Haven with nothing but oil, and latterly gas. But you will soon change your mind with a visit to Angle, tucked into the east of the harbour entrance. Whilst the views may be of ships and refineries, your immediate surroundings are beautiful bays, islands, forts, an unspoiled pub and a truly remarkable and understated 14th century tower house. A wonderful 3½ miles!

START Turn left off the B4320 at Angle to park in the car park by the shore at West Angle Bay (toilets and 'Dive-in' café). SM 854032.

1 From the car park walk with the sea to your left to climb around the north side of West Angle Bay. Ignore the first track to the left, but take the next (and visit the viewpoint if you wish). Now follow the distinct coastal path, which passes Thorn Island. *This was one of a series of forts built in the 1860s as part of the defences of Milford Haven, and which has now been converted into a hotel. Those familiar with Compton Mackenzie's tale Whisky Galore, based upon a ship laden with whisky which was wrecked on the island of Eriskay in the Outer Hebrides, should know that a similar event happened here, when the sailing ship Loch Shiel was wrecked on Thorn Island in January 1894. The crew were rescued by the local lifeboat, leaving 7000 cases of whisky aboard, a bonanza which proved to be too tempting for some. A father and son drowned whilst getting the liquor ashore, and another died from excessive consumption. Bottles were hidden everywhere – indeed two were discovered 60 years later when a cottage was being renovated. Divers still recover bottles today.* Go through a gate/stile and continue, enjoying a splendid view of the shipping activity and the north shore of Milford Haven.

2 Cross a gate/stile by Chapel Bay Fort, with its prominent gun, and carry on ahead. Cross another gate/stile and join a track which passes in front of a pair of cottages – numbers 1 & 2 Chapel Bay. Now just follow the obvious path over seven assorted gates and stiles until you arrive above the Lifeboat Station, which is painted pale green. Pass the RNLI container, cross the access road and walk into the hedged path to round Angle Point and cross another three gates/stiles to arrive at the charming **Old Point House** pub, having said hello to the resident goats. *This charming 15th century oak beamed inn is situated in an enviable waterside position, and still retains many original features. They specialise in fresh locally caught fish, and serve real ale.*

3 Continue beside the bay, passing The Ridge – *a spit where samphire grows* – to eventually pass by the church on your right, to join a road.

4 Turn RIGHT to walk back to your car along the main street of Angle. *This still has medieval field patterns extending either side, and contains 25 listed buildings. First visit St Mary's Church and the Seamen's Chapel. There were once three churches in Angle: St Antony's, near West Angle Bay and St Mary's at Chapel Bay are no longer there, but St Mary's thankfully remains. It was built in the 14th century, with the tower being added in the 15th century. It has a Norman font and 19th century stained glass windows. There is also a fine monument to the ancient families of Ferrers and Daws, who lived at Bangeston Castle, about a mile to the south-east. The charming Seamen's Chapel, which stands beside the church, is dedicated to St Anthony. It was founded by Edward de Shirburn, who was Knight of 'Nangle' in 1447. An effigy of Shirburn stands to the left of the doorway. The tiles around the altar match those in St David's Cathedral. The crypt was used for the many bodies of seamen once washed ashore here, recorded in the 19th century register as 'drowned'. Continue along the road, turning right by a*

Thorn Island

Hotel

West Angle Bay

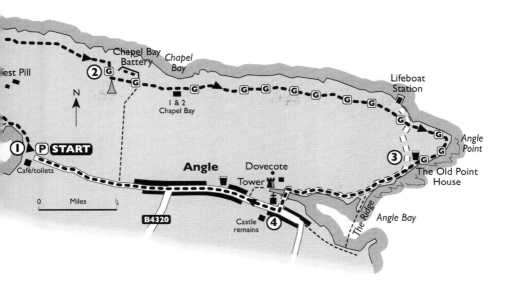

sunken garden and passing through a stile to visit the 14th century Tower House, where you can climb stairs to the top floor via the rounded stair turret. This medieval, once moated, mansion is a remarkable survival. It was occupied at one time by Edward de Shirburn of 'Nangle', who dedicated the Seamen's Chapel. This is Wales' only example of such a tower, and from here you have a good view of the nearby Dovecot. Return along the road to West Angle Bay, where you can enjoy a cup of tea at the café.

The Seamen's Chapel, Angle

WALK 14

NARBERTH MOUNTAIN

DESCRIPTION A 5-mile circuit which takes you close to the summit of Narbert Mountain, via the castle and some wooded cwms. A hilly return passes Heron's Brook, an ideal family venue, with authentic Punch & Judy shows, pony rides, 'pat a pet', lots of animals to see and the Forest of Myth and Legends. They also have an 18-hole approach golf course, as well as a pitch & putt. (*Open April to September*). Charge.
START Car park at Town Moor, Narberth. SN 108148.

I From the car park at Town Moor turn right and walk along the road to Market Square, passing the restored Town Hall. Continue ahead and, when the road bends to the right, turn LEFT below Narberth Castle. *Following the conquest of Pembrokeshire by Arnulph de Montgomery, the lordship of 'Arberth' was allotted to Stephen Perrot, who built a fortification on the summit of Camp Hill, just over half-a-mile south of the present town, around 1116. The present castle was built by Sir Andrew Perrot, his grandson, and garrisoned with Flemings. The town then grew around this site. In 1256 it was attacked and taken by Llewelyn ab Grufydd, but was eventually returned to the English crown. Having been repaired it came into the ownership of Sir Rhys ab Thomas and, in spite of damage sustained during Cromwells time, remained habitable until 1657. At that time it was part of the estate of the Barlows of Slebech who obtained permission to hold a market and fair in the town. The ruins have recently been restored and the castle is open to the public.* Now turn immediately RIGHT to pass through a stile. Continue along a path, passing through two stiles, and then another, and then a gate. Pass by the house Clubland to join a track, and continue.

2 At a T junction turn RIGHT then, after a short distance, turn LEFT. After about 25 yards leave the tarmac and fork LEFT along a track, with trees and a stream to your left.

When you join another track, turn RIGHT and continue AHEAD along this.

3 When you reach a minor road, cross it and continue ahead to reach a main road. Cross this and turn LEFT then, after about 20 yards, turn right up a minor road. *About a quarter-of-a-mile north of here is Allensbank, which was built in 1839 as the Narberth Union Workhouse, with accommodation for 150. It was built by J Thomas & Son of Narberth, and would have opened in 1838 had a mob not attempted to burn it down. Work continued with the protection of special constables, and a further delay occurred following a financial dispute with the builder. It was attacked in 1843 by over a hundred Rebecca Rioters, who were campaigning against road tolls. This time the Castlemartin Yeomanry provided protection. In 1930 it became a public assistance institution, and in 1948 a care home for old folk. It now privides attractive holiday accommodation.* You pass two farms and the surfaced track ends. Continue AHEAD.

4 When you reach an offset cross tracks, just before a radio mast, turn RIGHT to descend Narberth Mountain along Knights' Way. *In the 17th century Narberth Mountain was covered with 873 acres of woodland stocked with red deer. When you reach a road, turn RIGHT.* When the road bends right at Peter's Lake Bridge, look for a bridle way on the left (the sign is tucked away to the right) and turn LEFT. *If you wish to visit Heron's Brook, just continue along the road a little way – the entrance is on the right.*

5 Continue along the track and when you reach a road cross it, cross a stile and walk ahead to a bridge. Cross this, turn LEFT and follow a fence as it turns RIGHT. Cross a stile on the RIGHT, and then another, and then walk AHEAD, aiming just a little to the right of the summit of the hill ahead. Cross a stile and continue AHEAD, then veer left towards the church, now clearly visible. Cross a stile to the left of the church and walk AHEAD. Go through a gate and continue. When you reach the main road, turn LEFT to return to the start. *Narberth*

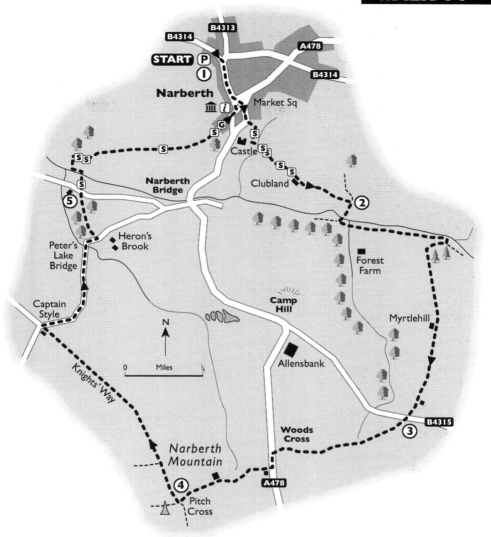

has officially been a market town since 1688, when James II granted its royal charter. It stands on the Landsker Border Line, which runs from Newgale in the west to the castle at Laugharne in the east, and separates the 'Englishry' of the south of Pembrokeshire from the 'Welshry' of the north of the county. The word 'landsker' is thought to be of Norse origin, and usually translates as 'frontier',

although it may actually mean 'a part of the country under foreign control'. Two trade routes crossed at Narberth, and the town became a venue for the drovers – St James Street was once known as 'Sheep Street' and the High Street was known as 'Pig Market Street'. Once the first stop for the Milford Haven to London stagecoach, it is still a busy and attractive location.

LAWRENNY QUAY

DESCRIPTION An absolutely stunning and very easy walk through beautiful oakwoods on the shores of the Daugleddau, with the added bonus of a charming and historic church to visit. 2½ miles.

START Park considerately near the entrance to the church in Lawrenny. SN 017069.

and walk along the shore. When you reach the road turn RIGHT to return to the village, the church and the post office/café. *St Caradoc's church, one of Pembrokeshire's finest, gives a clue to this village's prosperous past. Dating from the 12th century, it is dedicated to St Caradoc, the son of wealthy parents who was employed as a musician at the court of Rhys ap Tewdr. He is buried at St David's Cathedral. St Caradoc's has a Norman font and two 'squint' windows, to allow the the congegation to see the altar during mass. The south transept was built in the 14th or*

1 From the entrance to the church turn RIGHT and walk down the lane signed to Lawrenny Quay, passing the wreck of a sailing barge. *The large stone quay here reveals the village's trading past, with coal and lime being shipped, amongst bricks and other goods. Limekilns once stood by the waters' edge, and ferries ran from Cosheston and Houghton.* Follow the path past the yacht station and landing stage and then turn RIGHT, passing craft on hard-standing. Turn LEFT in the boat park and follow the track AHEAD.

2 Cross a stile to enter a wonderful National Trust oak woodland beside the Daugleddau. *These woods were once associated with Lawrenny mansion, which was demolished in the 1950s (its walled garden still survives).* Follow this narrow path as it winds through Lawrenny Wood.

3 When you reach a stile cross it and descend steps to the waterside at Garron Pill. *The head of Garron Pill was used in the 19th century for the export of lime from nearby quarries.* Turn RIGHT

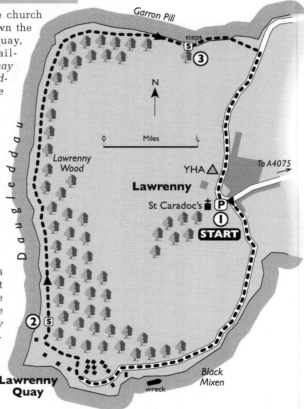

15th century and contains the stone figure of a knight. The post office/café makes a very good stop for a refreshing cup of tea, and some cake.

WALK 16
BOSHERSTON & ST GOVAN'S

DESCRIPTION This lovely 4-mile route visits the remarkable St Govan's Chapel, which stands just above the beach at the bottom of 75 steps. You then enjoy expansive views from St Govan's Head before returning beside the tranquil waters of Bosherston Lily Ponds. *This route enters the* *Castlemartin Firing Range area – you are advised to ring 01646 662367 after 16.30 the day before you visit to check access. Obey ALL notices displayed regarding the range.*

START Park in Bosherston National Trust car park (toilets). SR 966948.

1 Turn RIGHT from the car park and then LEFT to walk through the village. Ignore a road which branches to the left and continue AHEAD to reach the car park by the Ministry of Defence range entrance.

2 From this car park walk past the sign towards the sea, veering right to visit St Govan's Chapel and Well, which are at the bottom of 75 steps. *Inside the tiny chapel is a fissure, said to show the imprint of St Govan's ribs. He died in 586 AD and is said to be buried under the altar.* Return to the top and turn RIGHT, to walk with the sea to your right, and pass through a gate to follow the coastal path. *A diversion to St Govan's Head is well worthwhile if you have the time – the views are excellent.* The path passes through a gate, and continues to cross a stile, eventually descending steps to Broad Haven beach and its sands.

3 Walk across the back of the beach, veering LEFT to reach a footbridge. Cross this and continue AHEAD, ignoring a path to your left, to walk around the waters at Stackpole Warren. Cross a footbridge, turn LEFT and continue. Cross a second footbridge and continue. Eventually you reach a third footbridge, which you cross to follow the path back to the car park. *The Lily Ponds are flooded limestone valleys, at their best in June. Large pike and tench attract fishermen here.*

Map labels:
St Michael & All Angels'
START
To B4319 & Pembroke
St Govan's Inn
Bosherston
fort
Lily Ponds
Stackpole Warren
Dunes
Dunes
Dunes
Mere Pool
Broad Haven
Trevallen
Star Rock
Artillery Range
N
Miles
New Quay
Trevallen Downs
75 steps
St Govan's chapel & well
Long Matthew Point
St Govan's Head

31

MANORBIER & PRIEST'S NOSE

DESCRIPTION Starting between a romantic castle and a lofty church, this route takes you past the King's Quoit, overlooking Manorbier Bay, to Priest's Nose. A short stretch of steep and broken coast is then walked to bring you to Conigar Pit, where you turn inland by the army camp and its dilapidated collection of disused weapons. You then cross open land to return to the village – a 3-mile outing.

START Park in the car park (toilets) beneath Manorbier Castle, on the road down to Manorbier Bay. SS 062977

I Leave the left hand side of the car park to walk seawards – *you are soon overlooking Manorbier Bay, a west-facing beach popular with surfers.* Pass Kings Quoit – *a cromlech more remarkable for its situation than structure, and spectacular splits in the rock by Priest's Nose –* to follow the Coastal Path. The rocky coastline is spectacular. You cross a stile by Presipe and follow the clear path across a field to a stile by Manorbier Army Camp. *To your right is Conigar Pit, a former rabbit warren.*

2 Cross this stile and walk with the wire boundary fence on your right. Cross a stile, turn RIGHT and soon cross another stile as you walk around the perimeter of the camp. *Manorbier is now the main UK Close Air Defence (CAD) range for the British Army. RAR Manorbier is used to fire various CAD missiles, area–defence machine gun systems up to 35mm calibre, and provides firing and training facilities for all CAD units of the Field Army and Commando Forces. The Range is also used by the Defence Air Warfare Centre. There is a large danger area around Manorbier – approximately 220 square miles, out to a maximum of 13 miles at sea, and up to 50,000 feet overhead.* Carry on – *with army paraphernalia – trucks, old missiles and so on –* behind a wire fence to your right. Cross a stile to join a road and

turn LEFT. Follow this road as it swings right and then left.

3 Just beyond the '30mph' signs and before a children's play park, turn LEFT, cross a stile and follow the course of an old concrete road. When you reach the hedge, turn LEFT and soon cross a stile. Turn RIGHT, cross another stile and continue AHEAD. Cross one more stile and carry on. The path makes a minor zigzag but maintain your direction to join a road and return to the village. Turn LEFT to return to your car or, better still, right to call at the pub. You should also visit the castle and the church.

Manorbier Castle *This remains remarkably well-preserved, having only been subjected to two quite minor assaults – by Richard de Barri in 1327, and in 1645 by Cromwell's Roundheads. As with so many such castles it has its origins in a wooded hall and earthwork, and was built on land granted to the Norman knight Odo de Barri in the latter part of the 11th century. His son began building the stone structure early in the 12th century, parts of which still remain. It is renowned as the birthplace of Gerald of Wales (Giraldis Cambrensis, Gerald the Marcher) in 1146, who recorded descriptions of contemporary life, and described the castle thus: [it has] 'excellently well defended turrets and bulwarks, and is situated on the summit of a hill extending on the western side towards the seaport, having on the northern and southern sides a fine fish-pond under its walls, as conspicuous for its grand appearance, as for the depth of its waters, and a beautiful orchard on the same side, enclosed on one part by a vineyard, and on the other by a wood, remarkable for the projection of its rocks, and the height of its hazel trees. On the right hand of the promontory, between the castle and the church, near the site of a very large lake and mill, a rivulet of never-failing water flows through a valley, rendered sandy by the violence of the winds. Towards the west, the Severn sea, bending its course to Ireland, enters a hollow bay at some distance from the castle; and the southern rocks, extended a little further north, would render it a most excellent harbour for shipping... This country is well supplied with corn, sea-fish, and*

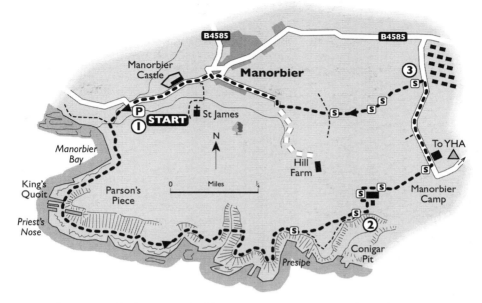

imported wines; and what is preferable to every other advantage, from its vicinity to Ireland, it is tempered by a salubrious air...'. The de Barris owned the castle until 1359, following which it changed hands several times and eventually became part of the monarchy's estate in the late 15th century. Queen Elizabeth I sold it to the Bowens of Trefloyne in 1630. Following the Civil War it was sold to the Phillips' of Picton in 1670 for the then very large sum of £6000. The estate, including a farm, orchard, fish ponds, dovecote and deer park was leased to J R Cobb, antiquarian and castle lover, in the late 19th century. He undertook a substantial restoration before it passed to the present owners. It is open Easter to September 10.30-17.30. Dogs allowed on a lead. Picnics welcome. Charge.

St James Church A church on this site was visited by Gerald of Wales, who worshipped here, and took refuge when Tenby was attacked by Welsh princes. The chancel is known as the 'weeping chancel' – it is said that a representation of Christ's head upon the cross can be seen on the wall. The present building dates from 1840, and enjoys a splendid positiuon overlooking the bay.

Manorbier Castle

WALK 18
TENBY TOWN

DESCRIPTION One of Britain's favourite seaside resorts, and quite justifiably so. With splendid clean beaches, a picturesque harbour and an intimate walled town up on the cliffs Tenby will reward a thorough exploration. This 1½-mile route visits most of the notable sights – including the Tudor Merchant's House and the Museum, passes some enticing pubs, the Town Walls and the charming Fisherman's Chapel. So don't rush around the route – take your time to fully enjoy this charming resort.

START St Julian's Chapel by Tenby Harbour. SN 005136.

Start by St Julian's Chapel, known as the Fisherman's Chapel, at Tenby Harbour.

The original Fisherman's Chapel used to be situated at the end of the old stone pier, where waves often broke over the building with such severity that the clergy from St Mary's, who led the services there, often refused to officiate. When they did, they were paid for their services with fish. Having fallen into a sorry state in the 17th century, it was used for the storage of fishing gear. The pier was rebuilt in the 1840s the chapel was demolished, and for a while the fishermen had to walk up to St Mary's, where they were not made welcome by many of the congregation, who found them to be 'smelly'. They also played cards and told jokes in church, much to the displeasure of the Rector, George Huntington. So in 1874 he decided that the chapel should be rebuilt, and money was quickly raised. Built using stone quarried on Caldey, the chapel was dedicated on St Andew's Day 1878. Walk up Penniless

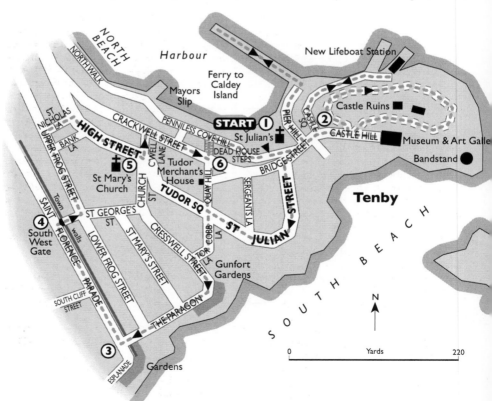

Cove Hill and turn LEFT to walk down Pier Hill. Visit the pier. Go back up Pier Hill and turn LEFT into Castle Square and continue, to visit the Lifeboat Station. *This brand new lifeboat station was completed March 2005, and stands on the site the old Royal Victoria Pier. It cost £5 million to build, and houses the first Tamar class boat to enter service with the RNLI. This 16-metre craft replaces the Tyne class lifeboat, introduced in 1981, and has a top speed of 25 knots, rather than the Tyne's 17 knots.*

2 Leave Castle Square and turn LEFT up Castle Hill to visit the castle remains and Tenby Museum & Art Gallery. *The museum & gallery was opened in 1878 in what was once an old National School building built in the 1830s and converted into a museum by local builder Lewis John at a cost of £44.12s.4d. The displays include local history, archaeology, maritime and social history, a pirate's cell, a Victorian antiquarian's study and a medical hall chemist's shop. The gallery has a permanent exhibition of works by brother and sister Gwen and Augustus John. Augustus, relaxing on the beach at Tenby, wrote: 'Gwen and I, full of curiosity, would approach as near as we dared, to watch the mystery of painting. Even at that early age we were vaguely aware of Art and Beauty'. Also work by local artists and visiting exhibitions. It is open 10.00–17.00 daily (closed winter weekends). Charge. There is not a great deal left of the castle, which was attacked by Llewelyn the Last in 1187 and again in 1260, and was quite ruinous by the 14th century. It was held under siege for 10 weeks during the Civil War.* Leave Castle Hill, walk along Bridge Street and turn LEFT into St Julian Street. Continue as it curves to the right, and turn RIGHT to visit the Tudor Merchant's House (NT) in Quay Hill. *This National Trust property will give you an insight into the life of a prosperous 15th-century merchant. It is a three-storey building with a large Flemish chimney and fireplace, and three of the walls contain original frescoes. The small garden to the rear is an accu-*

St Catherine's Island

rate recreation of a Tudor herb garden. Open April to October 11.00-17.00 (closed Sat). Now retrace your steps to cross the road into Cobb Lane. Turn LEFT into Cresswell Street and then RIGHT to walk along The Paragon.

3 Turn RIGHT into St Florence Parade passing Gardrobe Tower and continue to the South West Gate. *Following the destruction of Tenby by Prince Llewelyn in 1260 it was decided to build far more substantial defences. William de Valance began this work around 1264. Edward III granted Tenby the right to levy dues on merchandise in 1328, and this provided funds to strengthen defences, and build the present five entrance towers. The walls were strengthened in 1457, and a ditch was excavated where St Florence Parade is now situated. The threat of the Spanish Armada resulted in yet more defensive works.*

4 Turn RIGHT to enter the old walled town, which looks like a souk, then LEFT into Upper Frog Street. Turn RIGHT along St Nicholas Lane and then RIGHT again into the High Street to visit St Mary's Church. *There was a church on this site in 1210, but only traces of this building survived rebuilding at the end of the century, probably following the destruction of Tenby by Prince Llewelyn in 1260. The new building had a 83 ft high tower, and was enlarged further during the 15th century as Tenby's prosperity increased. Have a look for the amusingly carved bosses in the chancel roof, depicting mythical beasts, face-pulling and a mermaid with a mirror and comb. The spire reaches a height of 152 feet. The sacristy is said to be haunted by the ghost of a member of the clergy of the reformation period.*

5 Cross the road and walk down Crackwell Lane into Crackwell Street. Enjoy a fine view of the harbour as you turn RIGHT.

6 After a short distance turn LEFT down Dead House Steps to Penniless Cove Hill, passing the old mortuary. Turn RIGHT to return to the harbour and St Julian's Chapel, *enjoying views of St Catherine's Island and Caldey Island.*

WALK 19

SAUNDERSFOOT HARBOUR TO MONKSTONE

DESCRIPTION Don't be discouraged by a slightly inauspicious start to this 3-mile route – it soon develops into a lovely wooded coastal walk, with excellent views and a surprisingly attractive return route. If you have children with you, *TAKE GREAT CARE* at the viewpoint over Monkstone Point and Beach.

START Park in Saundersfoot Harbour car park (charge, toilets). SN 137048.

▌*An atmosphere of happy holidays, ice cream and sun hats belies the earlier life of Saundersfoot Harbour which was, from the late 18th to the early 20th centuries, a busy port exporting high quality coal and anthracite from the Begelly, Kilgetty, Thomas Chapel and Bonville's Court collieries, and iron ore from Wiseman's Bridge, which was linked by a tramway running along Railway Street, now known as The Strand. To the west of the harbour the name Incline Way recalls a time when wagons were brought down to the harbour from Bonvill's Court colliery using an inclined plane. It all came to an end just before the outbreak of the Second World War, and now the town is largely residential, with an infux of holiday-makers during the summer months.* Walk along the pavement of the B4316, which climbs to the south of the harbour, turning LEFT into 'The Glen'. When this road swings right, continue AHEAD onto a path, which climbs, sometimes steeply, into woodland. Stay with the main path, enjoying the occasional fine sweeping view over Saundersfoot Bay. Eventually the path descends to a waymark post by a 'V'-shaped footbridge. Remember this point for your return. Cross the bridge, pass the fenced-off mine shaft and carry on, climbing steeply.

2 When you reach a gate, go through and turn LEFT, keeping the hedge on your left. Go through a gate and continue, then another gate and descend a narrow path. At a path junction with a waymark post carry on ahead, then turn RIGHT for a very fine view of Monkstone Point and Beach, and distant Tenby. *THIS VIEWPOINT IS DANGEROUS – KEEP CHILDREN WITH YOU AND TAKE CARE. The beach at Saundersfoot suffered from oil pollution when the Sea Empress ran aground at the entrance to Milford Haven in 1996 (see* **Walk 12**)*, but there have been many other more benign shipwrecks (unless you were a member of the crew!) around Saundersfoot harbour and Monkstone Point, including the 'Victory', bound for Ireland with a cargo of coal in 1818; the sloop Cornwallis' in 1832; the 'Durham', a collier brig, in 1839; the 'Nautilus', a sloop, in 1854; the 'Policy', a brig, in 1859; the 'Martha', a sloop in 1867; the 'Anne', a sailing ship from Aberystwyth in 1872; the 'Masterpiece', a fishing ketch operating out of Tenby in 1901; the steamer 'Fermamagh' in 1938 and the 'Iliad', a sailing boat wrecked in 1961.*

3 Follow the path up to a five-way way-mark post and turn RIGHT, then descend to the next junction and turn LEFT to retrace your outward route for a while.

4 When you reach the 'V'-shaped bridge and mine shaft take the path heading inshore, away from your outward route, to walk through Rhode Wood. When you reach a track 'T' junction turn LEFT and continue. Go through a gate and continue ahead, ignoring a track on the right. Turn RIGHT at the next junction and then RIGHT again. Carry on ahead to reach a road.

5 Carefully cross the road, turn RIGHT and then fork LEFT up a waymarked track. When you join a road continue ahead. Look out for a prominent telegraph pole on the right-hand side, and when you reach it turn RIGHT down a path beside it to eventually enter Saundersfoot Plantation Community Woodland. Walk through the woodland to emerge at a road. Turn LEFT then immediately RIGHT to walk down St Brides Lane. At the end of the lane cross the road to the pavement and turn LEFT to return to the start.

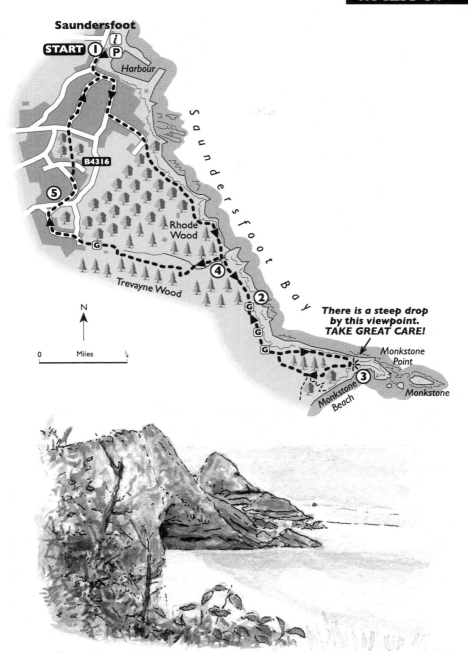

Saundersfoot

START ①

Harbour

B4316

⑤

Rhode Wood

Trevayne Wood

④

②

S a u n d e r s f o o t   B a y

N

0   Miles   ¼

There is a steep drop
by this viewpoint.
TAKE GREAT CARE!

Monkstone Point

③

Monkstone Beach

Monkstone

Monkstone Point

WALK 20
AMROTH & COLBY WOODLAND GARDENS

DESCRIPTION An excellent 3-mile walk visiting the National Trust (NT) Colby Woodland Gardens and returning via Green Plains and Sunnybank Farm for sweeping coastal views. The final ½-mile takes you along the grassy cliff tops west of Amroth, with a dramatic descent to the shore. The car park stands approximately on the site of a row of cottages swept away in the storms of 1931. The toilets were built on the site of Cliff Cottage, similarly destroyed.

START Park in the sea-front car park at Amroth, by the toilets, opposite the Cartwheel Restaurant. SN 162070.

1 *The car park stands approximately on the site of numbers 1-5 Beach Cottages. Their survival depended upon the mood of the sea, and finally they succumbed to its fury in 1931, having first been undermined by the strong tidal stream which sweeps the bay. If your visit coincides with low spring tides you will see the stumps of a submerged forest revealed – fossilised nuts, antlers and animal bones, along with Neolithic flints, have been found.* From the car park, walk with the sea to your right, turning LEFT uphill at the Amroth Arms pub. Continue, ignoring a road on the left, but then forking LEFT by 'Upper Mead' and continuing ahead along a wide, clear track. At a track junction, carry on ahead but, at the next path junction, fork RIGHT (don't cross the bridge!).

2 Go through a metal gate into NT Colby Woodland Garden. Ignore a bridleway which heads uphill to the right and continue ahead. You reach the NT shop, reception and café (01834 811885). *If you wish to explore the gardens you MUST pay your entrance fee – a visit is heartily recommended. The gardens are open 10.00-17.00 daily from late March to the end of October, and contain one* of the best collections of rhododendrons and azaleas in Wales There is also a new themed sculpture trail and excellent tea room. You continue ahead to emerge at a road. Turn LEFT, pass the entrance to Colby Lodge and fork LEFT along a track. Shortly you reach a track crossroads where you continue ahead and uphill, soon zig-zagging over rock. Ignore a path curving to the right and carry on uphill along a cosy hollow lane. Join a track and eventually emerge at a road.

3 Turn RIGHT and then, after about 25 yards, turn LEFT through a metal gate where 'organic meat for sale' is advertised. By the entrance to Cwmrath Farm go through a wooden gate on the LEFT and walk along another picturesque hollow lane. When you are faced with two gates, go through the LEFT-hand one and continue along the hollow lane. Cross a stile and turn LEFT to eventually emerge at a road.

4 Cross the road to the stile opposite and cross it, then cross another stile and walk along the right-hand side of a field (if there are cows here, calmly ask them to move!). Cross a stile in the field corner and carry on along a hollow lane, to finally cross a stile and turn RIGHT. Pass houses, go through a gateway and carry on along the track, enjoying a fine view of Saundersfoot. Cross a cattle grid and stay on the main lane, turning LEFT between bungalows and carrying on to eventually emerge at a road. Turn RIGHT.

5 Walk carefully around the bend in the road – *taking care with any traffic* – then turn LEFT into Meadow House Holiday Park. Walk straight ahead to eventually emerge through a wooden gate. Continue with a fence to your left to cross a stile, descend steps and turn LEFT to walk on a pathway cut into the green sward, enjoying a sweeping view to the east. Look out for a stile on the RIGHT: cross it, turn LEFT and carry on. *There is now a fine view of Caldey Island to your right.* Go through a gate and start to descend through woodland – when the track splits go LEFT. Descend more steep steps to return to the parking area.

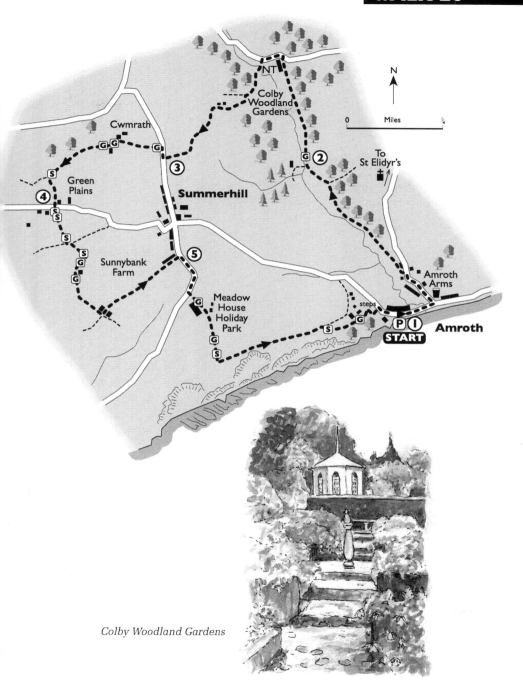

N

0   Miles   ¼

NT

Colby
Woodland
Gardens

Cwmrath

G G

G

③

Summerhill

Green
Plains

④

S

S

S

S

G

G

S

G

Sunnybank
Farm

⑤

G ②

To
St Elidyr's
✝

Amroth
Arms

steps

S

G

P ①
START

Amroth

Meadow
House
Holiday
Park

G

S

Colby Woodland Gardens

PRONUNCIATION

These basic points should help non-Welsh speakers

Welsh	English equivalent
c	always hard, as in cat
ch	as in the Scottish word loch
dd	as th in then
f	as f in of
ff	as ff in off
g	always hard as in got
ll	no real equivalent. It is like 'th' in then, but with an 'L' sound added to it, giving 'thlan' for the pronunciation of the Welsh 'Llan'.

In Welsh the accent usually falls on the last-but-one syllable of a word.

KEY TO THE MAPS

- —— Main road
- ═══ Minor road
- •➤• Walk route and direction
- ① Walk instruction
- - - - Path
- 〰 River/stream
- Ⓖ Gate
- Ⓢ Stile
- △ Summit
- 🌲🌳 Woods
- 🍺 Pub
- Ⓟ Parking

THE COUNTRYSIDE CODE

- Be safe – plan ahead and follow any signs
- Leave gates and property as you find them
- Protect plants and animals, and take your litter home
- Keep dogs under close control
- Consider other people

The CroW Act 2000, implemented throughout Wales in May 2005, introduced new legal rights of access for walkers to designated open country, predominantly mountain, moor, heath or down, plus all registered common land. This access can be subject to restrictions and closure for land management or safety reasons for up to 28 days a year.

Published by
Kittiwake Books Limited
3 Glantwymyn Village Workshops, Glantwymyn, Machynlleth, Montgomeryshire SY20 8LY

© Text & map research: David Perrott 2007
© Maps & illustrations: Kittiwake 2007
Drawings by Morag Perrott

Cover photos: *Main* Overlooking Abereiddy; *inset* Tenby Harbour. David Perrott

Reprinted with minor updates 2007 – 2013.
Printed by MWL, Pontypool.

ISBN: **978 1 902302 50 8**